All Scripture references taken from the KJV of the Holy Bible, unless otherwise indicated.

OPPONENT, ENEMY, OF ADVERSARY: *FIGHT THE RIGHT BATTLE WITH THE RIGHT WEAPONS*
by Dr. Marlene Miles
Freshwater Press 2025
freshwaterpress9@gmail.com

ISBN: 978-1-967860-58-6

Paperback Version

Copyright 2025, Dr. Marlene Miles

All rights reserved. No part of this book may be reproduced, distributed, or transmitted by any means or in any means including photocopying, recording or other electronic or mechanical methods without prior written permission of the publisher except in the case of brief publications or critical reviews.

Table of Contents

Opening Prayer 5

Introduction 6

In the Bible 15

The Enemy 26

Warfare for Opponents, Adversaries, & Enemies 30

The Frenemy: Camouflage, Not Confusion 36

Not Every Battle Is the Same 43

Not All Opposition Is War 46

The Opponent — Lessons from the Arena 50

The Adversary — When Resistance Has Assignment 55

The Enemy — When the Attack Is Personal 61

How to Discern Who Is Who 69

How God Uses All Three for Your Growth 75

Weapons for Each Battle — How to Respond . 82

Prayers, Declarations & Activations for Every Level of Opposition 89

12 Declarations for Daily Warfare 93

When the Enemy Is in You — Self-Sabotage, Inner Opposition & the War Within 95

Final Warning: Do Not Become What You Fight 99

Declaration 102

Battle versus War 103

Battle versus War — Seeing the Bigger Conflict 106

Battle versus War 108

Scriptural Warfare Against Enemies 116

Dear Reader 124

Prayerbooks by this author 126

Other books by this author 128

OPPONENT, ADVERSARY or ENEMY?

Opening Prayer

Lord, teach me to see clearly.
Give me Wisdom to discern who is sent to challenge me, who is sent to hinder me, and who is sent to destroy me.
In every battle — keep my heart clean, my spirit sharp, and my weapons correct.
In Jesus' Name. Amen.

Introduction

What is the difference between an enemy, an adversary, and an opponent? There is danger in mislabeling battles and those who come to bring battles into your life. Wolves in sheep's clothing are enemies in disguise who want to be mislabeled; this way they can do what they cam to do against a person. It is the desire of the ruthless enemy to be obscured or hidden. It is kingly of us to search out the matter, to see who has come to oppose us, who are they, what are they working with, why have they come? And it is incumbent upon us to know how to handle such oppositions.

Some Christians over-spiritualize everything. Well, life is spiritual so we should look deep into things that happen in our lives. Still, some Christians under-spiritualize everything, often saying, "It don't take all that." Well, it depends on who you are, where you come from, what your people did and may still be doing as to how much it will ***take***. It depends on all that as to if you can simply be saved and be at ease in Zion.

Good for you. I can't.

Not knowing that you have an enemy or who your enemy is, really—*if* he is an enemy, he could just be an opponent or an adversary. But if you don't know that a conflict has started, you might be in confusion. That's an enemy tactic, actually and it leads to wasted energy, wrong prayers, broken relationships, and it can lead to defeat.

To know if it ***takes*** all that, or what it actually takes requires that we know the difference between discernment and paranoia. From my book, **Discernment: The Unabridged Guide,** *"Spiritual discernment is a spiritual gift. It is the ability to distinguish between truth and falsehood, in both the natural realm and also in spiritual situations."* Discernment is a gift of God and like many skills, gifts, talents and abilities it must be used and it is sharpened by use. Paranoia, on the other hand, is a thought process but it is weighted by anxiety, fear, and suspicion. So, everything is suspicious, everyone is suspicious; that is not discernment, that is prejudice.

I've met people who say that everyone they meet is thus and so, until proven otherwise. I do not disagree with that person since they may know the lifestyle or qualities or lack of qualities of everyone that they meet. The main person that I've heard say this, I believe is full of sharpened discernment, as well as people-experiences, so I respect him. However, I cannot say or believe that everyone of a certain race or color is one way, versus another; that is prejudice. <u>All</u> men cannot be grouped into a category, and <u>all</u> women also cannot be contained in a category. Saying or thinking that all people of a certain background cannot cook, sing, dance, or jump is also prejudiced. Pre-judged is not discernment.

Discernment applies to the individual, an individual circumstance, and at a certain time. Spiritual discernment is seeing what there is to be seen, spiritually. We can use certain data and truths from the Word of God. For example:

> The devil comes not but to steal, kill, and destroy. (John 10:10)

Regarding the verse above and many other Truths in the Bible, you can wait to decide if it is true for yourself--, even over and over, or you can believe the Word, believe God, based on the fact that God cannot lie. Therefore, to be wise, we get our truths and facts from the Holy Spirit, even in real time, because He cannot lie. The Holy Spirit is where discernment comes from. He can bring Scriptures and verses to our remembrance and also, if we listen, He will talk to us. Yes, in real time.

> For we wrestle not against flesh and blood, but against principalities, against powers, against the rulers of the darkness of this world, against spiritual wickedness in high places. (Ephesians 6:12)

The Holy Spirit, who is all Spirit helps us discern because what we need to discern is often spirit, not flesh and blood. Discernment divides that human component from spiritual to tell us things such as what spirit or spirits are influencing the person that we are looking at or dealing with right now? Without spiritual discernment we may focus on the natural, what do they look like, sound like? What are they wearing? Do they look nice? Do they look rich or poor? We may then lean on our own understanding, which is natural, physical, and experiential, and then fall right back into prejudices. We may think every person who looks or sounds like this that I've met, seen, heard about, or dealt with is *just like this*. And we may be a thousand percent wrong.

The first level of what we may call conflict may come by way of the Opponent. By Wisdom, knowledge, understanding and discernment, we can know if an opponent has come into our situation. In its proper context, the opponent may engage us in a neutral or structured conflict. Typical arenas where we see an opponent in daily life are in sports, debates, elections, courtroom, games. Funny how we welcome that when we are the spectator, but we don't like an opponent very much when we are engaged in the battle.

The thrust of this is that you are on opposite sides *for the purpose of a contest*. Contests and conflicts are quite different things, usually. You and your opponent may even respect each other. The conflict is *situational and temporary*. When the event ends, the opposition ends.

No personal malice is required.

Examples include, the person running against you in an election. the other team in a basketball game.

Phrase test: "If we weren't in this competition, we could probably have coffee."

An Adversary is the next level up and it is different. In a normal context, the adversary brings ongoing resistance or opposition. Typical arenas include: Strategy, warfare, litigation, or power struggles.

The Key idea is that someone is *actively working against your goals, plans, or progress*. Not necessarily personal hatred, but intentional obstruction. May be long-term and strategic. Can be cold, calculated, or professional.

Examples may include: A rival corporation trying to crush your business, a lawyer on the other side of a lawsuit. Or, someone who wants to see your plans fail, even if they don't want to destroy *you* personally

Phrase test: "You don't have to hate me to stop me." You also don't have to want to stop me just because you hate me; you could live and let live, but that is not how an adversary thinks. If they thought like that, they'd just be a hater—a hater who takes no action against you.

> Be sober, be vigilant; because your adversary the devil, as a roaring lion, walketh about, seeking whom he may devour: (1 Peter 5:8)

And then there is the enemy. He has hostile, personal, or destructive intentions. We see an enemy in arenas such as war, betrayal, revenge plots and personal vendetta. If you know such a person who can't forgive anything or anyone, you should either stay clear or be sure not to anger them, because you are not off limits to their jealousy and rage. No one is.

The key idea is that someone wants *your harm, downfall, or destruction.* Their issue is not just with what you are doing, but their issue is with *you.* The conflict is personal, moral, emotional, or existential. They may attack openly or secretly. They are not satisfied until you are diminished, defeated, or gone.

Such an enemy could be someone who wants to ruin your reputation, your marriage or your entire life. Such a person could pit their kids against your kids. Without discernment, you know nothing about it—maybe even for years, but they are interfering with or trying to ruin everything good for your kids out of simple jealousy of your children, or because they hate you, and you may not be discerning that. For example, when a nation at war with another nation; they are out for total destruction or for takeover. A person who feels your very existence is a threat and may be petty to the nth degree.

When a person doesn't just want to stop another, they want to hurt them or worse, they are an enemy. They have no limits. It is as though they have no conscience.

Opponents have a low level of emotional investment in the contest; they only want to win. Usually there is respect from either side to the other side. The Adversary has a moderate level of emotional investment in the contest. Their goal is to block and defeat. There may or may not be respect between the two parties. The enemy escalates the emotion; it is high. His goal is to destroy or eliminate. Perhaps even for a lifetime. There is rarely respect for the intended victim by the perpetrator.

Now, you could see how an opponent, in the natural can start out as an opponent, but over time, without Jesus, they could advance into something darker such as an adversary, or something more dangerous, such as an enemy. By discernment, we must know what and who we are dealing with to properly deal with it.

Biblical literary shades of meaning—the average o*pponent is the* other runner in the race. And ad*versary is* the accuser in the courtroom" (like Satan in Job). The e*nemy is coming for blood; they could seek after the life of another, such as* Saul pursuing David.

In the Bible

Opponent, Adversary, or Enemy? Let's put a Biblical lens on spiritual & human conflict. When dealing with an opponent, it is more of a clash of assignment, rather than identity. In a Biblical sense, an opponent is someone on the *other side*, but not committed to your destruction. Using a word picture, think of a race, contest, debate, courtroom, duel.

An opponent opposes. That is, he sets, puts or lays, or thrusts obstacles (or himself) against a purpose, an outcome, or even against another person. An opponent is something or someone that opposes; opposite; adverse. One that opposes; particularly, one that opposes in controversy, disputation or argument. It is sometimes applied to the person that begins a dispute by raising objections to a tenet or doctrine, and is correlative to defendant or respondent. In common usage, however, it is applicable to either party in a controversy, denoting any person who opposes another or his cause. *Opponent* may sometimes be used for adversary, and for antagonist, but the word does not necessarily imply enmity or bodily strife.

An opponent is not a rival or competitor; it is something different.

I went to a church where a woman there opposed everything I said or was about to say. It was the weirdest thing. In adult Sunday School. If the teacher asked a question that required a response, most would sit quietly. After some pause I may raise my hand and choose to answer. I am not kidding, before I could form my first word, her head would snap toward me, and she was then planning to oppose whatever I was going to say before even hearing what I was saying because I had not yet begun to speak. I could say a Bible verse such as, **"For God so loved the world…"** She would have a comment or a retort, but most often she would start with, "No, that's not true." Now, what's even weirder, is that no one else noticed her behavior toward me. No one.

Okay, so if I quoted a verse wrong, and this woman is guarding the Word, then she would be my opponent, like an iron sharpening iron sort of thing. But I didn't misquote or misuse the Word so there was nothing to guard. She had escalated this from opponent which would have been my first estimation of who she was in this situation, to something more--, either adversary or enemy.

It took a couple of weeks, but I soon figured it out, she liked the fellow who invited me to that church--, she saw him first, must have been her rationale, but I was there with him, so she was trying to prove something. She didn't do this to anyone else to show herself as a know-it-all; she did it only to me in that particular classroom setting. So, this has become personal to her. I am not counter-opposing her, I am forgiving and being kind and gracious toward her. Then I would avoid her. Mistakenly, I stopped answering questions in Sunday School and I should not have done that.

Later, I left that church when I moved from that city. this woman who was never friendly to me--, like at all, began reaching out to me on LinkedIn, over and over, to invite me to dinner. *What?!* We weren't friends, and I thought

LinkedIn was for business, not dinner invites. But, at that time, I was only on LinkedIn and not on any other online platforms. Anyway, I thought maybe she wanted to apologize, but what if she, instead wanted to escalate? Nope. Not touching that with a ten-foot pole.

This interaction may have started out with her choosing to be my opponent, although I was not also *her* opponent, but escalated to adversary or whatever else was in her head.

Now, we reach a very sensitive place, your opponent may be opposing you because they are assigned spiritually to do that, or they have assigned themselves against you in their own contest, but you are not also their opponent. You've met people who are competing with you, but you have no idea that they are competing with you, *right*?

The same can be true in adversarial relationships and with enemies. It doesn't mean that you don't have discernment – well, at first, it may mean that you have no malice, no guile, no competition spirit with them or against them, no jealousy, covetousness, and no plots of revenge. So, you don't think *like that*. You don't prejudge—thinking everyone is *after* you because you are hot stuff and they are not. It means you are not paranoid, Praise the Lord! But it may mean that it could take a minute while you size up what's going on and turn on your sharp discernment so you will properly navigate this situation.

It may simply mean that you are comfortable in your own skin and you are not trying to get into or under theirs.

Scripture uses games, contests, and races as spiritual metaphors. Paul uses athletic metaphors to describe struggles that are *not personal*:

> Do you not know that in a race all the runners run, but only one receives the prize? (1 Corinthians 9:24)

> I have fought a good fight, I have finished my course, I have kept the faith: (2 Timothy 4:7)

Here, others in the race are *opponents*, not adversaries or enemies. Well, they shouldn't be, but true sportsmanship has taken a hit in these days and times. In some sports stadiums opponents play on the field, but when the fans in the seats take either winning or losing too far, sometimes fights break out and normal people temporarily become adversaries. It's a game, *man*. We can all take lessons from the stadiums and arenas where we are supposed to be enjoying sporting events. But even as humans, if we prepare and prepare for war but never go to fight it, sometimes fights break out in strange places like football stadiums, hockey games, or maybe even church pews.

Joseph's brothers turned themselves into opponents, but later became allies. Before that, it could have been that they could have escalated to adversaries or enemies, but they didn't kill Joseph, they sold him into slavery. The brothers did move from adversarial positions to that of enemies when they tricked and then attacked the entire city of Shechem, killing all the men and taking the women and children as captives to enslave them.

David versus Goliath was not personal--, well not at first, but then it became destiny-level. Goliath couldn't destroy the people of God, else how would the Davidic Covenant ever be fulfilled? When an antagonist is after your destiny, it has become personal. They are now your enemy.

The uncomfortable truth is that opponents are necessary for excellence. For example, in the workplace, ministry, sibling rivalry, and in leadership roles it is considered that some competition makes for improved performance, bettering both the contestants. I play a game online and I have been entered into a competition with others. It is annoying to me. I am not competing with those people; I don't even know who they are and if I did, I'm not playing a game to compete with them. It's a game. Please.

Jesus calls people to argue their case with honor. Argue and then agree.

> Settle matters quickly with your adversary who is taking you to court. Matthew 5:25

The opposition is real, but not evil, not destructive. We are not even supposed to rail against dignities. That means that even in spiritual warfare we are not disrespectful to the powers or entities that we are praying about. God made them all—even the fallen angels. If God is allowing them, then we follow protocol in prayers, warfare and even when speaking about such of God's creation. Ultimately, God will judge, so as in the natural, if we are in a Court of Law when we are in spiritual warfare and prayers, we are in the Courts of Heaven, therefore we behave ourselves with decorum. Now, whether the other side conducts themselves well or not—we do what the Word says and we should not take the provocation of evil or anything from the dark side.

In a story, for example, we might see two gladiators, or rival knights in a tournament. In daily life there may be another coworker competing for the same promotion that you desire. All things are done decently and in order as you vie for that position within your company where you work.

Still, spiritually, not every disagreement is demonic. The takeaway from this is that not everyone against you is *against* you

There is danger in not recognizing an opponent as an opponent, an adversary as an adversary, and an enemy as an enemy. If you treat an opponent like an enemy, for example, you create unnecessary warfare.

The adversary brings structured and intentional resistance. This word, *adversary* has a Hebrew root: *satan*. "one who opposes, accuses, obstructs." Important: *Before Satan was a name, it was a job description. Satan is a job description; it is a group who behave in the same evil way.*

In the Book of **Job**, Satan is "the adversary," the one who **accuses and resists**:

Then Satan (the adversary) came also among them. (Job 1:6)

Using that definition based on the Hebrew root: *śāṭān* = one who opposes, we see Job's accuser, Nehemiah's mockers, Paul's "thorn." This is the "spirit of sabotage."

Opponents and adversaries can reveal weak spots, motives, and immaturity. These antagonists could be *used by God* to refine you. (We will go more into that later.) But know this, everyone is not your enemy; some are actually "your exam."

An adversary is an opponent or foe; it is one who speaks against another, a complainant, and specially the devil who roams about like that roaring lion. (1 Peter 5:8), and where Satan is called the adversary by way of eminence.

An adversary is an enemy or foe; one who has enmity at heart. Know this: The Lord shall take vengeance on his adversaries. (Nahum 1), and since we are in covenant with God, His enemies are our enemies and our enemies are also His enemies.

An adversary is an opponent or antagonist, as in a suit at law, or in single combat; an opposing litigant. Remember Jesus said to agree with them quickly. However, the adversary is not just disagreeing; he is attempting to block, test, and frustrate. In 1 Kings 11:14, God "raises up an adversary" *against* *Solomon* because of disobedience. This adversary is a strategic hindrance, not an emotional hater. In court language, the adversary is the prosecuting attorney.

In a story, the adversary is the rival kingdom trying to stop you from building. In life, it is someone working behind the scenes to sabotage a plan. Spiritually, it is Satan (or a satan) as "the accuser of the brethren" (Revelation 12:10)

The key idea is that an adversary attacks your *purpose*, not necessarily your *person*. You fight opponents with skill. You, in turn, must fight adversaries with strategy and discernment.

> But if thou shalt indeed obey his voice, and do all that I speak; then I will be an enemy unto thine enemies, and an **adversary** unto thine adversaries. (Exodus 23:22)

Lord, stir up an adversary against my adversary, in the Name of Jesus. (1 Kings 11:23)

He is near that justifieth me; who will contend with me? let us stand together: who *is* mine adversary? let him come near to me. (Isaiah 50:8)

The adversary hath spread out his hand upon all her pleasant things: for she hath seen *that* the heathen entered into her sanctuary, whom thou didst command *that* they should not enter into thy congregation. (Lamentations 1:10)

Lord, bend Your bow against my enemy and my adversary, in the Name of Jesus. (see Lamentations 2:4).

Lord, avenge me of mine adversary. (Luke 18:3)

The Enemy

The enemy is different than the opponent and the adversary and far more dangerous. He is personal, relentless, and destructive. By definition, he is someone committed to another's downfall, harm, or extinction. From the Bible we see these terms as coloring an enemy, hatred, vengeance, wickedness, war, betrayal, assassination.

An enemy is a foe with a certain level of dedication to their evil. A private *enemy* is one who hates another and wishes him injury, or attempts to do him injury to gratify his own malice or ill will. A public *enemy* or foe, is one who belongs to a nation or party, at war with another.

One who hates or dislikes; as an *enemy* to truth or falsehood is an enemy. In theology, and by way of eminence, the *enemy* is the Devil; the archfiend. In military affairs, the enemy is the opposing army or naval force.

When the attack is personal, that's an enemy attack. Bible examples include:

David versus Saul - Saul became David's enemy continually. (1 Samuel 18:29)

This is not competition. It is obsession. Saul wants David removed from existence, as much as Cain wanted Abel removed from the Earth.

Herod versus Jesus - Herod sought the young child to destroy Him. (Matthew 2:13)

Herod exterminated all the male children under two years old to try to kill baby Jesus. That is enemy-level evil: destroy the person and their destiny.

- Haman versus the Jews. Haman wanted to exterminate all the Jews in a genocide.
- Judas versus Jesus – Judas' betrayal was to destroy Jesus.

Yet, Jesus teaches: *Love your enemies.* (Matthew 5:44). Not "love your opponents," not "love your adversaries, but your enemies--, the ones who want to hurt you. In a story: the villain who wants you dead, not just defeated in life: the one who resents your existence, not just your position is your enemy--, perhaps even your arch nemesis.

Spiritually: Satan moves from accuser to murderer (John 8:44). So you can see how he can influence others to do the same.

Prayer:
Lord, give me discernment to know who is competing with me, who is resisting me, and who is seeking to destroy me — and give me wisdom to respond in the right way, and in the right spirit. In the Name of Jesus. Amen.

General references to enemy or enemies may be found in the following verses, for your future study. Exodus 23:5; Job 31:29-30; Psalm 35:1-28; Proverbs 24:17-18; Proverbs 25:21-22; Matthew 5:43-48; Luke 6:27-36; Romans 12:17, Romans 12:20.

The wickedness of David's enemy is seen in, Psalms 56:5; Psalms 57:6; Psalms 62:4; Psalms

69:4, 9; Psalms 71:10; Psalms 102:8, Psalms 109:205; Psalms 129:1-3.

Imprecatory prayers against enemies will be listed next. An imprecation is a spoken curse. These are the Psalms that are imprecatory or judgmental. They call down or invoke the judgment of God, or calamity on enemies. Psalms: 69 and Psalm 109 are considered the main two. Additionally Psalms 5, 6, 10, 12, 35, 37, 40, 52, 54, 55, 56, 57, 58, 59, 79, 83, 94, 137, 139 and 143.

Instances of forgiveness of enemies can be found in the Bible, especially since Jesus taught it:

- David, of Absalom and co-conspirators (2 Samuel 19:6; 2 Samuel 19:12-13)
- Jesus, of His persecutors, (Luke 23:34)
- Stephen, of his murderers, (Acts 7:60)

Warfare for Opponents, Adversaries, & Enemies

There are three different levels of antagonists, and there are three different spiritual responses. How to respond, how to fight those who come up against you:

For three levels of conflict, three levels of Wisdom are needed to respond properly. The opponent attacks your goal, so you respond to him with skill, discipline, steadfastness. Use self-control and excellence as weapons against your opponent.

The adversary is against your progress. So, respond to him with strategy and discernment. Your weapons of choice will be Wisdom and prayer. The enemy is the most dangerous; he is after your identity or even your very life. You respond in your divine authority in warfare. Put on all the armor of God. Now, if appropriate use love and forgiveness as weapons, but you still may have to do battle. But be sure you are not warring against people, but against spiritual wickedness in high places. If there is any unforgiveness in you, it could inhibit your success in the warfare.

Confusion is the enemy's first victory. If you mistake an opponent for an enemy, you will waste energy. If you treat an enemy like an opponent, you will be destroyed. So, break out your discernment so you can be clear as to what and who you are dealing with.

BONUS: "Discern the Difference" Prayer

Lord, show me who is an opponent, who is an adversary, and who is an enemy. Let me not mislabel people or mismanage battles.
Give me spiritual x-ray vision.
Let me respond to each level with the correct weapon and the right heart.
In Jesus' Name. Amen.

Prayer for Opponents 1

For those who are in competition or disagreement, but they are not evil.

Father, in the Name of Jesus,
thank You for the grace to recognize that not every opposition is an attack.
Give me the maturity to walk in self-control, excellence, and integrity.
Help me win without hatred and lose without bitterness.
Let me honor You in every contest of life — spiritual, professional, relational.
May I never turn a natural opponent into a spiritual enemy through pride or offense.
Teach me to compete without corruption and to disagree without dishonor.
Let my light shine even in rivalry, so that Christ is seen in me. In Jesus' Name.
Amen.

Key Scriptures: 1 Corinthians 9:24, Proverbs 27:17, Romans 12:18

Weapon: Discipline, character, excellence

Posture: Remain calm, strategic, respectful

Prayer for Adversaries 1

For those who intentionally resist, accuse, or sabotage you.

Lord, my Defender and Judge,
I thank You that no weapon formed against me shall prosper and every tongue that rises in judgment *I shall condemn.*
Expose every hidden plan, every false accusation, every silent sabotage.
Give me wisdom like Nehemiah, strategy like David, and discernment like Daniel.
Teach my hands to war and my mind to stay sober and alert. Silence the voice of the accuser. Block the strategies of the opposer.
Turn every adversarial plan into an unintentional promotion. Let everything meant to stop me *strengthen me* instead.
I do not fight flesh and blood — I fight by Spirit, wisdom, and truth. In Jesus' Name. Amen.

Key Scriptures: *Job 1–2, Psalm 27, Isaiah 54:17, Nehemiah 4*

Weapon: Strategy, discernment, prayer, legal authority in the Spirit.

Posture: Remain watchful, wise, unmoved

Prayer for Enemies 1

For those who desire your destruction, downfall, or elimination.

Mighty God, Warrior of Heaven,
You are the God who delivers from lions, giants, and assassins.
I stand under the Blood of Jesus Christ.
I cancel every plot of destruction, every curse, every assignment of hatred.
I reject fear, retaliation, and vengeance —
for the battle is not mine, but Yours.

I forgive by force of will, even if my feelings are not ready.
I release my enemies from my hands,
but I place them in *Your* hands — the hands of the Righteous Judge.

Where they curse — bless me.
Where they dig pits — let them fall into them.
Where they plan evil — reverse it into deliverance, promotion, and testimony.
Let the snare of the fowler be broken.
Let every devil behind the enemy be scattered by Your fire.

Protect my life, my name, my destiny, my family, my assignment.

Let no enemy triumph over me.

In the Name of Jesus. Amen.

Key Scriptures: *Psalm 35, Psalm 91, 1 Samuel 18–24, Matthew 5:44, Romans 12:19*

Weapon: Forgiveness + spiritual authority + angelic defense.

Posture: Peaceful in spirit, lethal in the Spirit

The Frenemy: Camouflage, Not Confusion

Faithful are the wounds of a friend; but the kisses of an **enemy** are deceitful. (Proverbs 17:6)

Not all opposition is war. Some opposition is to make you stronger. Weights in the gym – is that war, or is that opposition to increase your strength? When we are sent opposition, it most often is uncomfortable. It is different. And it takes work. The first key is to discern what is this? *(Who dat?)*. Who *sent* it? What is its purpose. Things like refining fires and pruning don't feel so great, but we must grow in the Lord and Amen. I'd rather the Lord send me something to help me grow than for an adversary or enemy to come into my life, especially unawares, or unprepared.

There are people who are not fully friend and not fully foe. They come in a cloud of confusion and plan to spread that cloud, that confusion as far as they can. The confusion they create is not accidental. A frenemy survives by living in the gray space between affection and opposition. They stay close enough to qualify as "safe," but far enough in motive to function as a threat. They can be male or female. They could be pretending to be in a romantic relationship with you, but they have either been sent or they have some nefarious motive. But you may be all bubbles and flowers and happy as can be, but they are on assignment.

So, there can be boy frenemies and girl frenemies.

Most believers mislabel frenemies because they judge interaction, not intention. But in spiritual discernment, behavior is never the full truth, agenda is.

A frenemy is not always loud, but they can be. A frenemy is not always hostile. A frenemy is not always jealous in the obvious way. But those who always want to know what you have or what you are getting, even where you are going and who are you going to be with, are often frenemies, (akin to witchcraft). But a frenemy is always watching, always comparing, and always measuring how your progress affects *their* identity.

What Makes a Frenemy?

A frenemy is someone who needs and usually gains access to you, because you gave them that opening. They use it in order to feel superior to you. Expect them to compliment you publicly but compete with you privately. They most likely will act supportive while quietly gathering information. They will appear harmless but function as a slow drain to your confidence. Some frenemies are spouses. They may disguise critique as "concern. " they will stay close, not because they love you, but because they need proximity to stay relevant.

A true friend celebrates your wins. A frenemy studies your wins. An enemy plots against your wins.

When you realize what's going on, the real question is not, "Why are they like this?" but "Which battle category do they belong in?" A frenemy can fall into any of the three levels:

- If they just want to outdo you, then they are an Opponent.
- If they want to weaken or block you, then they are an Adversary.
- If they want you removed or ruined, they are your Enemy.

A frenemy is not a *type* — they are a mask. The real identity is <u>behind</u> the friendliness.

Again, we must visit the danger of prejudging, misjudging, not discerning or ignoring completely. If we misclassify this could be costly. If you treat a frenemy like a true friend, you give them:

- Access they haven't earned, and will use against you.
- Influence they shouldn't have.
- Information they can weaponize later

Have you ever had the long- or short-term friend or relation that you have confided in, only to have them completely turn on you and tell everything you told them in confidence to everyone you know? Well, you know, that was a frenemy. Their goal in doing this will tell you their level.

If you treat a frenemy like an enemy too early, you look unstable, and they get to play the victim; and they will play it to the hilt. That's why the Bible doesn't say, "Be harmless as doves and blind as puppies.. No, it says:

> Be wise as serpents, and harmless as doves.
> (Matthew 10:16)

Wisdom protects. Naivety exposes. Frenemies are not confusing, by they bring it. They will have you questioning yourself instead of them. Until you wise up and fully discern. Frenemies are not confused; they are strategic

A frenemy studies you to see:

- How much you trust
- How much you reveal
- How much influence they still have
- When to activate their true intentions

They do not need to destroy you today. They just need to stay close enough to strike efficiently later. Judas didn't betray Jesus at the beginning of the relationship. He waited for the moment of impact.

How to Disarm a Frenemy Without War

You don't have to call them out. You don't have to expose them to others. You don't have to "fight" them. You simply reclassify them. Reclassification is not war, it is Wisdom. Declassify them; take away their "special clearance" to have access to you, your marriage, your family, your ministry, your business--, your life.

Once you change the category, the relationship resets:

- Opponents are observed, not confided in.
- Adversaries are restricted, not debated with.
- Enemies are prayed over but never empowered.

The most powerful response is not confrontation. It is *clarity*. Clarity does not end every relationship, but it ends the illusion of the relationship.

Activation Question:

"Is this person, no matter who they are, or who they think they are in my life—even if they are a relative or a romantic interest, ask the question. Are they good for my growth — or just for their own advantage?"

How you answer that determines whether they're a friend... an opponent... an adversary... or an enemy in disguise.

Not Every Battle Is the Same

There is a great deal of unnecessary warfare in the Body of Christ — not because the enemy is so powerful, but because the people of God do not always understand *who* they are fighting, *why* the resistance came, or *what level of battle they are actually in.*

Too many believers are swinging swords at situations that only require self-control. Others are fasting against people they should simply forgive. Some are calling people "demonic enemies" when the only thing truly under attack is their own pride. And worst of all, many are completely unprepared for *true* spiritual enemies because they wasted all their energy fighting opponents and adversaries like they were devils.

There is a difference between someone *against your idea*, someone *against your progress*, and someone *against your life.*

The Bible does not use one word for all opposition. It gives us distinctions: **opponent, adversary, and enemy,** because not all resistance requires the same response.

- You do not rebuke an opponent.
- You do not negotiate with an enemy.
- You do not underestimate an adversary.

When you confuse the category, you choose the wrong weapon.

Some people in your life are **opponents** — they are simply on the other side of a decision, assignment, or opportunity. You don't need deliverance from them. You need discipline, wisdom, and maturity.

Some people are **adversaries** — they are sent to resist, accuse, block, or oppose what God has assigned you to build. They do not need to be hated, but they *must* be discerned.

And some people — or *spirits* working through people — are **enemies**. Their goal is not disagreement, not delay, but **destruction**. They do not want you corrected; they want you gone.

This book is about learning to discern the difference. The truth is simple, but dangerous to ignore:

"When you mislabel the threat, you mismanage the battle."

There is a cost for treating an opponent like an enemy — you lose relationships God sent to sharpen you.

There is a cost for treating an enemy like an opponent — you will be blindsided and devoured. There is a cost for treating an adversary like a friend — you will hand them tools they will use against you.

- Discernment is not suspicion.
- Discernment is not cynicism.
- Discernment is wisdom in war.

This book has been written to teach you how to fight the right war with the right weapon — and allow you to refuse to be destroyed by what you don't understand.

Not All Opposition Is War

If you live long enough, you will discover an uncomfortable truth: **the presence of opposition does not always mean the presence of evil.** Some opposition is spiritual. Some opposition is human. Some opposition is developmental — sent by God to mature you. Some opposition is self-inflicted, created by your own impatience, pride, or fear. You can probably think of some trouble that found you because of your own choices or actions. For example, you stepped in a mud puddle and got water and mud all over your shoes. Well, you could have waited until it stopped raining, or you could have gone the long way around, but you were impatient and decided to jump the puddle but didn't jump far enough.

The untrained believer sees opposition and immediately declares, "The devil is attacking me!" The mature believer pauses long enough to ask, "What kind of opposition is this? And why is it here?"

This can also be seen in the dream state. A person could wake up from a dream that seems horrendous, frightful, scary. But after praying and listening to the Holy Spirit you may find that even though the dream was dramatic, it was God's way of telling you something, but He had to get your attention. The drama of the dream was simply meant to grab your attention and tell you to pay attention. Thank God if a scary dream turned out to be nothing big in the natural; it may be a sign to look at yourself. Perhaps you over dramatize things, and this is God's way of showing you that a little thing in the natural was a big thing in your dream.

Additionally, it could be success if you dreamed of something huge in the dream, woke up prayed about it and caused it to be diminished or become nothing at all in the natural. That was an example of using the right weapon to fight a spiritual problem that was shown to you in the dream. (More about weapons coming up.)

Not all resistance is warfare. Sometimes it is a classroom. Sometimes it is a mirror. Sometimes it is a test. Sometimes it is a promotion in disguise.

Every believer must learn that you **cannot fight everything with the same weapon.** You don't fast over someone who simply disagrees with you. You don't ignore someone who is actively trying to destroy you. You don't curse someone God is using to humble you.

Misinterpreting opposition will cause you to get exhausted fighting battles God never told you to fight. You may break relationships you were meant to grow from; in so doing, you may separate yourself from destiny helpers sent by God. You may invite spiritual warfare where only emotional maturity was needed, such as when someone says or does something that really bothers you and you go into full blown anger or rage when you should have remained calm and or just walked away. That could have been a test, and you could have failed it. Misinterpreting the situation, you could mistreat training as persecution.

When a person calls human conflict "demonic" and demonic conflict "human." That is because of confusion and spiritual blindness; the enemy loves this.

If God is allowing a thing, He is using it—and most often to your ultimate benefit. God allows opposition because iron sharpens iron. Look at how God uses antagonists in your life.

- Opponents sharpen your excellence.
- Adversaries refine your strategy.
- Enemies establish your authority.

Without opponents, you stay average. Dull, really, if there is no sharpening. Without adversaries, you stay untested. Without enemies, you stay un-anointed. That doesn't mean to serve adversaries and enemies tea; you still have to do the work and the warfare when it is indicated.

Opposition is not always proof that the devil is present. Spiritual testing is proof that God is preparing you for the next level.

The Opponent — Lessons from the Arena

Opponents are the lowest level of resistance, but they are also the most common. An opponent is not an enemy. An opponent is not a threat to your existence — only to your *position, advantage, outcome, or comfort.* An opponent is someone who stands on the other side of a goal, decision, position, or opportunity. They do not have to hate you to oppose you. They do not need to destroy you to defeat you. The conflict is situational, not personal.

In the Bible, opponents show up most clearly through competition metaphors. Paul uses athletic language repeatedly, not to describe warfare against demons, but the ***discipline required to fulfill a calling.***

"Do you not know that in a race all the runners run, but only one receives the prize?"
(1 Corinthians 9:24)

Opponents sharpen your ability, your consistency, and your focus. You do not *pray them away…* you *train because they exist.* You keep your body under, you resist the devil and he flees. You fast. You observe the disciplines of the faith. Observing disciplines is warfare in action, not just in words.

Opponents do not attack your character, your destiny, or your identity — they simply want to *win where you want to win.* They challenge your level of preparation. Daily we are being tested at the level that we should be at right now in our Christian walk based on when we got saved, not when we felt like acting like we got saved. If you got saved at 13 and now, you're 30, you are not going to get the baby tests that a teenager might get. You are going to get 30-year-old level tests designed for a person who has been saved 17 years. Opponents also expose a person's lack of discipline. I'm not saying that any pastor or deliverance minister is judging anyone, but they can see, based on your problem what you might not be doing in your Christian walk. If you ae not following the disciplines, you won't get the right result. I can see, based on those gums and where the cavities are on teeth if a person is flossing or not.

Opponents force you to improve your skill. They motivate you to operate at your best; you must rise. And opponents help keep you honest about your abilities.

Opponents are often people you could work with, respect, or even like, outside the moment of competition. They can be coworkers, classmates, siblings--, but not devolved into excessive sibling rivalry, business competitors, ministry peers, or even fellow believers. You're not in a *war*— you're in a *race*. The obstacles, hindrances, and possible delays in your race may not be the same as your pew neighbor, but you still must overcome what you must overcome to reach your milestones, landmarks and finish lines, in your own race.

Misnaming opponents can turn neutral people into enemies that they were never meant to be. A person can make spiritual warfare out of a natural disagreement by mismanaging the situation. Mislabeling could damage relationships God meant to use for growth. Praying a prayer you don't need can't hurt anything, but study, excellence, skill, change, and resistance could fix this latest opposition. Wrongly-called antagonism may cause a person to become combative in seasons that require focus, not fire. Some believers call everything demonic because they don't want to admit they need **self-control, education, discipline, or time.**

Unless the other team, your opponent is using witchcraft to defeat your team (or you), you don't bind the devil when the real issue is that someone else practiced more than you. (However, I have heard many stories about teams using witchcraft to defeat another team.)

Biblical Opponent Examples

- Jacob and Esau in the womb (competition, not hatred… well, not yet)
- Elijah versus the prophets of Baal *on Mount Carmel* (a spiritual contest)
- Jesus versus Pharisees in *public debates* (opponents until they shifted to enemy-level hatred)

When an opponent becomes jealous, bitter, or obsessed — they can evolve into an adversary or even a full enemy. But they may not have *started there*. In the example of the woman who opposed me in Sunday School, I had no reason and no Godly spiritual intel to believe that she hadn't escalated from opponent to adversary or enemy. Wisdom would not let me go to dinner with her to find out.

Key Lesson:

- Opponents build your competence.
- Enemies build your character.

An immature believer prays for victory without preparation. A mature believer trains for the test they *know* is coming.

The Adversary — When Resistance Has Assignment

An adversary is not merely someone on the other side; an adversary is someone who is *invested* in blocking your progress.

In Scripture, the word, *adversary* comes from the Hebrew word *śāṭān*, which to us is *Satan*. It means "one who opposes, accuses, or obstructs." Before Satan was a proper name, it was a job description. The adversary is not trying to win the same race, they are trying to stop you from running it at all. When you have something to offer, say in a classroom, work, or other setting, but the enemy has shut you up because you don't want to rock the boat, or have a fight with them--, they've won. They have shut you out of the race. When you have a sibling that wants you totally out of the family, I suppose, so they can shine or shine the most and you oblige because why would you want to spend your holidays with family only to be shunned or hurt, then the adversary has won. At least for now. But you are becoming more disciplined, stronger, and more discerning. You can again take your rightful place in your family of birth.

Adversaries resist movement, breakthrough, building, momentum, strategy, and progress. They don't just want a victory against you — they want *delay, frustration, collapse, or discrediting.*

Adversaries:

- Block plans
- Drain energy
- Accuse motives
- Question your competence
- Stir others against you
- Create confusion & distraction
- Attack reputation, not just results
- Try to make you stop — not just lose

Adversaries are often strategic, subtle, and persistent. They may not hate you, but they are committed to opposing what you are building--, be it relationships, career, business, ministry. They want you to come down off that wall and stop building.

Biblical Adversary Examples:

- **Satan with Job,** was not trying to kill Job, but to make him *curse God and quit.*

- **Sanballat & Tobiah vs Nehemiah** — not trying to kill him first, just stop the wall from being built.

- **Paul's "thorn"** — described as "a messenger of Satan sent to buffet me."

- **The accuser in Zechariah 3** — resisting Joshua the priest's right to stand before God.

Adversaries are **purpose-focused**: The issue isn't *you as a person*, the issue is the *assignment on your life*. When it comes to sibling rivalry, it could be the place and purpose that you are called to in the family. Look at Joseph. Everyone has their own assignment, but in jealousy, Joseph's older brothers coveted Joseph's anointing and destiny. I've seen families where one is the "chosen one" perhaps as the deliverer of a family, but the others fight him. They may not even know why. They will assign it some flesh value like, 'he thinks he's all that because of his job, his house, or his fine car, while the rest of us have less (or nothing'.

This is why adversaries show up when you start building, growing, or stepping into destiny.

The difference between an opponent and an adversary is that the opponent competes with you, while the adversary works against you. The opponent wants to win, but the adversary wants you to STOP. With an opponent, the conflict may be temporary while the adversary doesn't stop so the conflict is ongoing. The opponent doesn't need to or doesn't necessarily hate you, but the adversary hates you, doesn't like you and is simply not your friend.

What happens when you mislabel an adversary as an opponent? I've done this more than once, myself—you know, being a good Christian, being forgiving and tolerant. Being related – and your parents told you to *get along* with your siblings (or other relative). Hate to say it, but sometimes you must know by discernment, Wisdom, or otherwise when someone hates your guts, even if you don't hate theirs. What a shock to find out the relative you love the most doesn't share your same warm feelings of familial love toward you.

When you get it wrong and call it wrong, you underestimate the assignment behind the resistance, if you even see the resistance. You may explain it away as, 'oh, she's just playing with me.' Or, 'he didn't mean it.' You try to negotiate with what must be spiritually confronted. You trust too much, often exposing plans to someone waiting to sabotage them. They are brazen; they will ask you your plans with so much feigned care and interest. And there you go, just spilling all the tea. Or, you assume they will "come around" when they were never sent to agree with you. Instead, you waste time trying to win them when the real need is to outmaneuver them and do what God sent you to do.

The Purpose of Adversaries:

- To mature your *strategy*
- To expose your *naivety*
- To strengthen your *boundaries*
- To purify your *motives*

- To force you into *prayer-led planning*
- To push you into a higher level of building under pressure

Having an adversary is not a sign you have failed. They are a sign that **what you are building matters enough to be resisted.**

The Enemy — When the Attack Is Personal

An enemy is not simply someone who disagrees with you, competes with you, or resists you. An enemy is someone who desires your downfall, destruction, or elimination — whether physically, spiritually, reputationally, or emotionally.

An opponent wants to *win*. An adversary wants to *block*. An enemy wants to *erase*. An enemy does not just oppose what you do, they resent who you are. They are not threatened by your actions, they are threatened by your *existence*.

What Makes an Enemy Different?

- They do not want peace, only dominance or removal.

- They attack identity, not just activity.
- They recruit others into the fight.
- They do not get tired, they get more strategic.
- They do not apologize, they justify.
- They are not satisfied when you lose — only when you're gone.

Enemies are *not always loud*. Sometimes they move silently, smiling right at you while planning. Sometimes these enemies are spiritual, not even human. Sometimes the true enemy is using a human face as a mask. This is where household witches come in. The enemy needs an evil human agent to accomplish evil against a human. The jealous, bitter, competitive sibling or coworker is too often the choice. The closer to you the better.

Enemies rarely show up in your life until destiny becomes visible. If you've got a bunch of enemies, count it all joy, but get into the battle or the war, and win, to the Praise of God's Glory!

Biblical Enemy Examples (review)

Saul versus David - Saul was not just opposed to David's music, skill, or success. He wanted David **dead**.

> And Saul became David's enemy continually. (1 Samuel 18:29)

Herod versus Jesus - Herod did not want to debate Jesus. He wanted to kill Him *before He could speak a word or perform a miracle.*

> Herod sought the young child to destroy Him. (Matthew 2:13)

Haman versus the Jews - One man's offense became a genocidal obsession.

> If it please the king, let it be written that they may be destroyed… (Esther 3:9)

Judas versus Jesus - Real enemies begin as trusted ones — they need proximity to deliver betrayal.

This may be review, but it is so important that it must be driven home. The enemy targets your identity – who you are. He will make you doubt yourself, question who you are, and whose you are. He makes you question or doubt what you were born to do, and even if anyone even cares. The enemy will have you asking yourself, 'Is anyone even listening to me?' Or, 'what's the use?' He targets your reputation and most often will try to besmirch it. He attacks purpose, destiny and your legacy.

Enemies are destiny-sensitive. They show up when something in you becomes a threat to darkness, power, or control. They do not always oppose your present, your today; no, they often attack your *future*.

Now, lets go deeper: there are two kinds of enemies.

1. **Human enemies** – people who are driven by hatred, jealousy, offense, or demonic influence.

2. **Spiritual enemies** – principalities, spirits, generational assignments, demonic rulers. So the spiritual realm sends the spiritual enemy as well as influences the human enemy—but we don't fight against flesh and blood.

You can confront a person, but you fight a spirit. You can expose a betrayer, but you rebuke a devil. The mature believer learns to separate the vessel from the force behind it.

Jesus, while being killed by His enemies said, *"Father, forgive them, for they know not what they do."* There are people, under the influence of evil, under the influence of darkness who do things and they may know what they are doing because they've done it so much, or they've chosen it—whereas it did not choose them. They've chosen works of the flesh, repeatedly so they know what they are doing is evil, but they are getting some kind of morose satisfaction from it. Well, they think they will.

But what they probably do not know is the extreme level of wickedness of their act. They most likely do not know how much trauma and trouble will result from their choice. They may nearsightedly think it is only them and their chosen enemy and they want to win and even destroy the other person. But the cascade of evil that will befall their supposed victim and also themselves, will go into generations and generations. All this may not be known by the deceived, wicked, host of evil who is waging and raging against another person – most often a person of God.

When Jesus said, "Forgive them," that was not weakness, that was spiritual clarity because Jesus knew the whole picture.

When You Mislabel an Enemy:

- You underestimate the danger.
- You try to negotiate with someone committed to your downfall.
- You keep trusting someone who is gathering information to destroy you.
- You keep giving access to someone God is trying to expose.
- You pray *for comfort* when you should pray *for deliverance.*

When it comes to discernment, don't ignore those little inklings, that is discernment—teething. It could start as a little itch, it could feel uncomfortable, going against all you know in your mind and natural experiences, but it is discernment trying to grow teeth, trying to sharpen. Enemies require boundaries, warfare, and the justice of God.

The Bible does not say, "Be kind to your enemies and give them access." It says, "Love your enemies" — which means release vengeance to God, not partnership to them. And do not take revenge upon yourself. Most often when I have known a person has really wronged God and not me, but by me, I feel fear or sadness for them because I know God will act. It is sobering, *yes*?

Loving an enemy does not mean letting them stay close. It means refusing to let their hatred infect *you and drag you into the flesh*. Men get beaten up in the flesh, but if you stay in the spirit, you will be victorious.

Why God Allows Enemies:

- To reveal what was hidden.
- To activate your anointing.
- To shift you into your next season.
- To prove God is your defender.
- To expose that enemy-- their jealousy, treachery, and sabotage,
- To fulfill prophecy.

David would never have become king without Saul. Joseph would never have reached the palace without betrayal. Jesus would never have reached the Cross without Judas. The early church would never have spread without persecution.

Sometimes the enemy is the transportation system to one's destiny.

Key Lesson of This Chapter:

- Opponents sharpen your skill.
- Adversaries sharpen your strategy.
- Enemies sharpen your authority.

You do not *pray the same* against all three. You do not *fight the same* against all three. You do not *respond the same* to all three. To fight an enemy like an opponent is fatal. To fight an opponent like an enemy is foolish. To fight an adversary like a friend is disastrous.

How to Discern Who Is Who

This is a good time to ask, *"Who dat?"*

Discernment is not suspicion. Discernment is not paranoia. Discernment is not guessing based on emotion, offense, or past trauma. Discernment is **clarity from the Holy Spirit** about the true nature, role, and intention of a person, situation, *spirit*, or opposition. It is used for when you have to know that you know.

How to Discern Who is Who

There is an emotional discernment, it is in your memory. "The last time this happened to me, it felt like this." There is muscle memory and physical discernment. I hear it a lot, 'the last time my tooth felt like this, I needed a root canal.' Hey, every pain is not the same and every same pain is not the same thing, but they can be close.

And superior to all those types of discernment, there is divine spiritual discernment, it is from the

Holy Spirit of God. It is right, it is righteous, it is true, it is timely, and you need it.

As in medicine, or dentistry, ask the right questions, get truthful answers, make the right diagnosis. Following will be 4 diagnostic questions that will help you discern, *who dat?*

Universal Discernment Prayer

"Lord, show me who is who."

Reveal who is sent to sharpen me, who is sent to hinder me, and who is sent to kill what I carry.
Remove blindness.
Remove emotional fog.
Remove false loyalty.

Give me eyes to see, ears to hear, and a spirit that is not deceived.
In Jesus' Name. Amen.

This is the chapter where everything turns from *theoretical truth* to *practical wisdom*. If you cannot tell the difference between an opponent, an adversary, and an enemy — you may (except for the Grace and Mercy of God, use the wrong weapon. You may pray the wrong prayer. Misdiagnose the attack. Keep the wrong people close. Push the right people away. Destroy what was meant to develop you. Protect what was assigned to destroy you.

In the spirit, **mislabeling can be more deadly than the battle itself.**

Four Questions of Discernment: When someone resists you, challenges you, or comes against you, ask:

1. **What is being attacked?**

- My *position*? Then this is likely an **opponent**.

- My *progress?* Then this is likely an **adversary**

- My *identity, destiny or life?* Then this is likely an **enemy.**

2. **How personal is the opposition?**

- No emotion, just competition? Its an opponent.
- Emotion mixed with strategy? It's an adversary

- Obsession, hatred, or cruelty? It's an enemy.

3. Does this person stop when the situation ends?

- An opponent stops when the contest ends.
- An adversary returns whenever you advance.
- An enemy continues until you fall or disappear.

4. What do they stand to gain if I fall?

- Opponent wants the *position.*
- Adversary wants the *progress halted.*
- Enemy wants the *person removed.*

The most dangerous thing about lack of discernment is that you could be feeding what wants to kill you, while starving what was sent **to bless you.** You could mentor a Judas. You could be venting to a Sanballat. You might rebuke a Paul-in-training. You block a door God opened because it came with resistance. You let an enemy sit in the inner circle because they speak the right language--, maybe they know a few Bible verses, or they have a Jesus pin on their lapel.

Discernment is not just a gift for the prophetic — it is a survival weapon for *every believer.*

The Three Most Common Discernment Errors:

1. Calling an opponent an enemy - You destroy a relationship that could have developed you.

2. Calling an enemy an opponent - You underestimate what is trying to destroy you.

3. Calling an adversary a friend - You hand them the information they will use to block you.

You need the Holy Spirit. You think AI is smart? The Holy Spirit is smarter than all AI put together. Know this: you will *never* discern correctly by, guessing or analyzing behavior alone. Nor by Googling personality traits. Or listening to gossip. Neither by trusting vibes or first impressions, or by asking a bot. None of that is discernment.

The Holy Spirit reveals **intent, assignment, and origin.**

> The Spirit searches all things, yes, the deep things of God.
> (1 Corinthians 2:10)

> "You will know them by their fruit.
> (Matthew 7:16)

Discernment is *not judging prematurely* — it is seeing accurately before damage occurs.

A Discernment Activation Prayer

Lord, sharpen my spirit.
Teach me to see the difference between friend and foe, assignment and distraction, divine resistance and demonic resistance.
Remove emotional blindness.
Protect me from false loyalty, deceiving appearances, and misplaced compassion.
Let me hear what is not being said, see what is not being shown, and know what is not being confessed.
In Jesus' Name. Amen.

How God Uses All Three for Your Growth

One of the biggest spiritual shocks in a believer's life is the realization that **God does not remove every enemy, silence every adversary, or prevent every opponent. Saved or unsaved, life is not always comfortable.** Sometimes God *sends* opponents, adversaries, or enemies. Sometimes, God permits them. Sometimes, He *uses* them. Sometimes He will not deliver you *from* them, because He intends to deliver you *through* them.

Not all resistance is the devil's plan. Some of it is God's training. Not all warfare is punishment, some of it is preparation. Not all opposition is demonic; some of it is developmental.

There are battles you win by running, by rebuking, or by remaining still. But there are other battles you win by growing.

God can use opponents to build your excellence. An opponent is not sent to destroy you — they are sent to push you.

- Opponents sharpen skill.
- Opponents expose laziness.
- Opponents force discipline.
- Opponents remove excuses.
- Opponents measure capacity.
- Opponents reveal how badly you want it.

Opponents are not blockers, they are **barometers**. Without opponents, you stay average. Without someone else wanting the same thing, you'd never stretch. David, for example, didn't become a warrior by fighting Goliath, he became a warrior defending sheep against lions and bears, well before Goliath. The enemy, (Goliath) revealed what the *opponents* had already shaped.

God uses adversaries to build your *strategy & wisdom*. Adversaries do not attack your talent; they attack your progress, structure, systems, and advancement. You don't survive adversaries by emotion. You survive by discernment, planning, and prayer-led strategy. Nehemiah didn't fight Sanballat with swords he built with a plan. Job didn't argue with the devil, he endured with revelation.

You want to be drafted into a pro football league. Your workout buddy will work out with you, but then he will suggest that you go out on a eating and or drinking spree and do reckless things that will jeopardize what you are building.

Daniel didn't protest the lions; he outlived the conspiracy.

Adversaries teach you:

- How to build under pressure. Peer pressure is real pressure.
- How to pray with intelligence.
- How to watch and work at the same time.
- How to move in silence.
- How to fortify the weak areas of your life.

Without adversaries, you'd build recklessly. With adversaries, you build wisely. Without adversaries, when you get to the next high level, your next promotion, you'd have no experience that would keep you in your next level. (Okay, I said it, you can't be stupid and stay in positions of power and authority. You must both learn and be refined on the way up, so that no one can bring you down once you get there.)

So, you may now have the answer as to why God hasn't fixed this, or stopped this yet. You're still being perfected by the Lord.

God uses enemies to build your *authority & destiny.* So if the battle is fierce, if the enemy is ferocious, know that the growth will be immense and the promotion from God will be epic.

Enemies are the final proof that **you are carrying something worth killing.** Enemies do not come for hobbies, distractions, side hustles, or side projects. Enemies come for destiny. Ever so often I will post a You Tube teaching or prayer and the battle will be horrendous, seemingly relentless. This is when I know this particular upload is really important to someone, some people, and of course to God. Still, being the first partaker, it is surely to help me as well. Praise the Lord! I'd like to share that the warfare to post Christian content for all these years has been tremendous, but as soon as I post, I suddenly feel fine. It took me a while to see that the adversary was opposing my progress even to the point of sending evil arrows, that I finally learned to send back, in the Name of Jesus. Now, I don't have crazy symptoms or delays as much when creating and posting Christian content for global consumption.

- Saul's hatred pushed David into the throne God promised him.
- Haman's plot revealed Esther's calling as deliverer of a nation.
- Goliath didn't just threaten Israel, he announced David's arrival.
- The crucifixion didn't stop Jesus; it activated the Resurrection.

Your enemy is a prophetic announcement.

Enemies do not show up when you start — they show up when you're close.

Enemies confirm elevation. Enemies reveal hidden anointing. Enemies activate heaven's intervention. Enemies expose what hell fears most about you. Without enemies, you'd never know the **weight** of the oil on your life.

Summary: The Redemptive Purpose of Each Level. If the level of in the conflict is an opponent, then you use skill, excellence, and focus, just as Paul said he would run the race and finish his course. This leads to mastery.

If the conflict is brought by an adversary, then break out divine strategy and Wisdom, with persistence. This is how Nehemiah prevailed over Sanballat to reach completion.

If the conflict arrives via an enemy, then stand in your divine authority, knowing your identity, as David did versus Saul and you will receive promotion from the Lord. As well, you will reach destiny and leave a favorable legacy.

If God Allowed It, He Intends to Use It

Joseph said, "What you meant for evil, God meant for good."

Paul said, "A messenger of Satan was sent... a thorn in the flesh, that I not be exalted above measure."

Jesus said, "No man takes My life , I lay it down."

Some enemies are not there to kill you. They're there to **reveal you.** Some adversaries are not there to block you. They're there to **refine you.** Some opponents are not there to humiliate you. They're there to **elevate you.**

Key Insight for the Mature Believer:

A person can be used by hell, but the situation can still be used by Heaven. You do not have to thank the adversary. But you *will* thank God for the maturity, clarity, strength, and authority you gained because of them.

Weapons for Each Battle — How to Respond

Every level of opposition requires a different weapon. Every kind of resistance demands a different posture. Every attack is not a demon. Every conflict is not emotional. Every battle is not loud.

When you pick up the wrong weapon, you either:

- fight harder than the situation requires,
- or fight weaker than the situation demands.

The Kingdom principle is simple:

You do not fight everything the same way.

Jesus did not answer every critic. David did not swing at every spear. Paul did not rebuke every storm. Nehemiah did not negotiate every accusation. Esther did not expose Haman on the first day.

Spiritual maturity is not "always fighting." Spiritual maturity is knowing how to fight, when to fight, and what to fight with.

Weapon Sets for Each Level of Opposition:

If confronted by an opponent the wrong response is: Anger, pride. The right response is focus, excellence, and self-control. (1 Corinthians 9:24-27)

The wrong weapon for an adversary is emotional over-sharing, venting, telling the same old story over and over. The Word says that we can have what we say, so taking a script the enemy has given you and repeating it, even once, can be dangerous. Repeating it over and again can be devastating. Stop telling people what happened to you or what he or she said about it. Instead, be strategic, be watchful in prayers and in the words you speak. Your mouth is a weapon of warfare – careful how you use it. Set boundaries. (Nehemiah 4-6)

The wrong response when an enemy presents is trying to negotiate with them, trying to people please. DO NOT AGREE with them, no matter how intimidating they seem, how weak you feel, or how tempting their offer may seem. The correct response is spiritual warfare in your position of spiritual authority. If necessary and possible, take them to the Courts of Heaven and ask for divine Judgment and justice from the Lord. (Psalm 35, Ephesians 6)

Weapons for Opponents- Competition-Level Resistance:

Opponents do not require spiritual warfare. They require preparation, maturity, and mastery. Your weapon is discipline. Your strategy is improvement. Your posture is honor and self-control. Your prayer is "Lord, help me grow, focus, and excel, in the Name of Jesus."

You do not fast and speak in tongues for three days over someone who just outworked you. For example, athletes don't (normally) pray against the other runner. No, they train to run faster. If you fight an opponent as if it is a demon, you look foolish.

Weapons for Adversaries When There Is Sustained Resistance:

Adversaries are not impressed by your passion — they attack your planning. If your life keeps getting shot down in the planning phase – you have one or more adversaries. Your weapon is strategy. Your defense is discernment. Your posture is watch and build. This is where you must work smarter, not just harder. Guard your speech; don't tell your plans to everyone. Maybe, don't tell your plans to anyone, but God. Protect your plans. Partner prayer with Wisdom. Stop announcing everything publicly, especially on social media. Don't borrow trouble.

Refuse emotional distraction. Nehemiah never stopped building because of adversaries. No, he built *differently* because of adversaries.

So we built the wall... for the people had a mind to work. (Nehemiah 4:6)

If you fight an adversary with feelings, you lose. If you fight them with Wisdom, you win. Judge Judy won't even let a person defend themselves with feelings; it's just not admissible.

Weapons for Enemies (Total Destruction-Level Warfare):

Enemies are not trying to delay you — they are trying to *erase you*. This is where authority, intercession, and spiritual warfare activate. You do not negotiate. You do not explain. You do not "hope they calm down." You do not try to win them over with niceness.

You switch weapon, using:

- **The Blood of Jesus**
- **The Sword of the Spirit (Word)**
- **Binding and *loosing***
- **Ask God for angelic assistance**
- **Fasting**
- **Impregnable boundaries**
- **Hermetic seals: shut down all access to you, like Jericho.**
- **Forgiveness and repentance (to remove their legal doorway)**

Enemies require **war and restraint.** You fight them **in the spirit**, and you keep your soul clean.

Through You we will push back our enemies.
(Psalm 44:5)

No weapon formed against you shall prosper —
(Isaiah 54:17)

If you fight an enemy like an opponent, you die. If you fight an enemy like an adversary, you delay them. If you fight an enemy as an enemy, you end them — spiritually, not carnally.

Key Wisdom: **Silence Is a Weapon Too**. Opponents are defeated by *outperforming them*. Adversaries are defeated by *out-planning them*. Enemies are defeated by *outlasting them, by God's power*.

But in all three cases, there is one universal weapon: You do not explain your strategy to the thing trying to stop you, or stop your plans.

Practical Application:

Before responding, ask, "Is this a sword fight, a building season, or a race?"

Ask before speaking, "Am I about to reveal plans to someone who hopes I fail?"

Ask before reacting, "Is this an emotional attack or a demonic one?"

Ask before praying, "Am I asking God to remove what He *sent* or allowed to mature me?"

Prayers, Declarations & Activations for Every Level of Opposition

This is the chapter where understanding becomes warfare, and knowledge becomes authority. These prayers are not reactions, they are strategic responses matched to the level of conflict. Praying the wrong prayer for the wrong battle can be disastrous.

Prayer for Opponents 2:

This prayer is for when the fight is not spiritual, but developmental.

Father, in the Name of Jesus,
thank You for every person who challenges me to grow, sharpen, and rise higher.
Teach me to distinguish competition from attack, and training from warfare.
Give me the grace to win well and lose well.

Deliver me from pride, insecurity, jealousy, covetousness, foolish rivalries, and comparison..
Let discipline do its work in me.
Let excellence be my answer, not anger.
Make me a good steward of skill and opportunity.
And let me never confuse human rivalry with spiritual battle.
In Jesus' Name. Amen.

Activation declaration: "I do not fear competition. I rise through preparation."

Key verse to speak aloud: *"Run in such a way that you may obtain the prize."*(1 Corinthians 9:24)

Prayer for Adversaries 2:

This is for when resistance is strategic, intentional, and recurring.

Lord, my Defender and Judge,
thank You that no plan can succeed against Your purpose in my life.
Give me the Wisdom of Nehemiah — to build, watch, and pray at the same time.
Expose every hidden motive, sabotaging voice, and false leader, peer, and helper.
Let every trap backfire.

Let every whispering tongue fall to the ground.
Teach me when to speak, when to be silent, and when to shut the gates.
Turn their resistance into my refinement.
And let every delay become acceleration in my favor.
In Jesus' Name. Amen.

Activation declaration: "I do not negotiate with sabotage. I outlast it, outthink it, and outbuild it."

Key verse to speak aloud: *"Nevertheless we made our prayer unto our God, and set a watch against them day and night."* (Nehemiah 4:9)

Prayer for Enemies 2:

For when the assignment is to destroy, not just distract.

Mighty Warrior God: The Lord is a warrior, the Lord is His Name.
I stand under the Blood of Jesus Christ.
I cancel every assignment of destruction, disgrace, accusation, or death.
I release forgiveness to every human vessel —
but I bind the *spirit* behind the attack from working against me.

Let the snare of the fowler be broken.
Let every pit dug for me become the grave of the digger. Let the stone rolled against me roll back on the roller.
Let every curse sent toward me return void.
Let every demonic contract be annulled by the Blood of Jesus.
I decree: I will not be silenced, deleted, displaced, replaced, broken, or destroyed.
The Lord fights for me.
Let what was meant to end me elevate me.
In the Name of Jesus. Amen.

Activation declaration: "I do not die here. I rise here."

Key verses to speak aloud: *"The Lord is a man of war; the Lord is His name.* (Exodus 15:3) *"No weapon formed against you shall prosper."* (Isaiah 54:17)

12 Declarations for Daily Warfare

Speak aloud:

1. **I will not fight emotional battles with spiritual weapons, nor spiritual battles with emotional reactions.**
2. **I do not fear resistance — I interpret it.**
3. **I will not lose myself fighting what was sent to grow me.**
4. **I refuse to empower enemies with access, even if it means that I move into a season of silence.**
5. **I outlast attacks because I am not fighting alone.**
6. **My assignment will not be aborted by accusation, sabotage, or intimidation.**
7. **I am not confused. I am discerning.**

8. **Every level of resistance becomes fuel for my next level of anointing.**

9. **God trains my hands for war, my fingers to fight, and fills my mind with Wisdom.**

10. **I do not panic. I strategize, I pray, I prevail.**

11. **No enemy gets the last word over my life — God does.**

12. **What was sent to destroy me will testify for me.**

Victory Psalm (Read out loud)

Psalm 3 (NIV)

Many are my foes, but greater is the One who stands with me.
They plan, but the Lord overturns.
They accuse, but the Lord defends.
They threaten, but the Lord protects.
The snare is broken.
The trap is exposed.
The enemy is defeated.
And I rise — whole, wiser, sharper, anointed, and unafraid.
In Jesus' Name. Amen.

When the Enemy Is in You — Self-Sabotage, Inner Opposition & the War Within

Not every battle is external. Not every enemy has a face. Not every threat comes from the outside. Some of the greatest victories you will ever win are internal victories — the battles against the parts of you that resist growth, healing, obedience, consistency, and destiny.

You can defeat every opponent, outthink every adversary, and outlast every enemy, but if the inner enemy is not conquered, you will eventually sabotage your own success. This is the war most believers never identify — because it cannot be rebuked, blocked, or bound. It must be healed, disciplined, or crucified.

Types of Inner Enemies:

- Fear – talks you out of assignments before you even start.
- Pride offends you into isolation or rebellion.
- Insecurity – causes you to shrink where God said, "stand and Stand therefore."
- Self-doubt – Turns victories into luck moments, instead of identity.
- Trauma memory – reacts to new people as if they are the old danger. Break every soul tie to your past traumas.
- Comfort addiction – rejects growth because growth requires discomfort.
- People-pleasing – hands authority to those who don't even deserve it.

The Most Dangerous Enemy Is the One You Protect. David could defeat lions, bears, Goliath, and armies, but the battle he lost was **with himself**, in private, on a rooftop.

Samson could kill a thousand with a jawbone but he could not conquer the craving that led him to Delilah.

Saul could defeat Philistines, but he could not defeat jealousy.

Judas could cast out devils, but he never cast out greed.

The enemy outside of you is never as dangerous as the enemy inside of you.

Signs You're Fighting an Internal Adversary:

- You keep losing in the same area
- You kill momentum right before breakthrough.
- You pray for deliverance from cycles you continually repeat.
- You blame others for battles you created.
- You feel unworthy of what God called you to do.
- You sabotage relationships, opportunities, or blessings you actually wanted.
- Your pattern is louder than your intention.

Inner Warfare Is Discipleship + Deliverance + Discipline

Some inner enemies must be:

- **healed** through Truth. Truth is a deliverer.
- **starved** through discipline.

- **cast out** through deliverance
- **retrained** through new thinking
- **crucified** through dying to self

Not every enemy needs counseling. Not every enemy needs casting out. Some need *confrontation and responsibility*.

Inner Victory Prayer

Lord, deliver me from the version of me that resists You.

Break every inner agreement with fear, sabotage, shame, pride, and defeat.

Heal the root.

Close the door.

Rewire the pattern.

Let every part of me agree with destiny, not destruction.
In Jesus' Name. Amen.

Final Warning: Do Not Become What You Fight

Opposition can shape you — or deform you. War can refine you — or poison you. Enemies can elevate you — or turn you into a mirror of the very thing you survived.

This chapter is a sober reminder: **You can win the battle and still lose your soul.**

Saul became what he hated. The persecutor became a persecuted king. The one who hunted David died tormented by the very spirit he once defeated.

You can become:

- A champion who turns into a tyrant
- A survivor who becomes suspicious of every friend
- A victim who becomes a villain

- A warrior who becomes addicted to war
- A defender who becomes controlling
- A believer who becomes bitter defending the faith

The Greatest Victory Is Remaining Whole

It is possible to:

- Win and stay kind
- Confront and stay clean
- War and stay worshipful
- Carry scars and still love deeply
- Know danger and still trust God
- Reject evil without becoming hateful

The true test of warfare is not **did you win?** The true test is **who did you *become*** **while winning?**

Warning Signs You Are Becoming the Enemy:

- You fight everything, even peace.
- You trust no one, even the righteous.

- You keep score instead of keeping faith.
- You become obsessed with proving yourself right.
- You tear down more than you build.
- You need enemies to feel powerful. Some people just like to keep something going.
- You can no longer receive correction.
- You justify when you do what would've once grieved you, what you once criticized someone else about.

A wounded warrior is still dangerous — but a bitter warrior is *deadly*.

The Higher Victory

Be not overcome by evil, but overcome evil with good. (Romans 12:21)

Overcoming is not just defeating the enemy, it is refusing to become like him. Anyone can fight evil. Only the transformed can defeat it without reflecting it.

Do not desire the king's dainties...(see Proverbs 23:3)

Do Not Become What You Fight

Saul became what he hated. Satan was not born an enemy; he *became* one. Bitterness turns opponents into devils. There is an eternal danger of mismanaged warfare.

Declaration

I will not lose myself in battle.

I will not lose my relationship with God.
I will not become what I destroy.
I will not let war change my worship, my honor, my purity, or my God-given identity.
I will win *and stay whole*.
In Jesus' Name. Amen.

Battle versus War

There must be strategy beyond the fight in front of you. if what is in front of you has escalated from a battle to a war, then you are not just in a fight, you are in a campaign. You are not just attacked the enemy is planning to wear you down. You and your destiny are important to God, else the enemy would not care. The enemy is not just after a moment, he is after momentum.

Most believers know how to fight **a battle.** Let's talk about how to win **a war.** David vs Goliath was a battle. Saul coming against David, was a war. Elijah vs Baal prophets was a battle. Jezebel's campaign of exhaustion was a war.

Jesus versus temptation in the Wilderness was a battle, but the Scripture says that Satan left Jesus alone for a time, meant he was coming back. This meant that Satan was strategizing and planning to escalate into more battles. More than one battle is a campaign or a war.

The tactics of war are different from the tactics of battle. The battle is for quick victory; the war requires long endurance. The enemy wages war through cycles, through fatigue, through repeated accusations, through attrition—a slow eroding, wearing the flesh of a man down. The enemy further uses *familiar spirits* and patterns, distractions and delays. He wages war against man through long-term erosion of faith, confidence, identity, will.

Christians lose the war even after winning the battle sometimes. This could be because:

- They fight hard but don't rest

    But now the LORD my God hath given me rest on every side, *so that there is* neither **adversary** nor evil occurrent. (1 Kings 5:4)

- They pray but don't plan.

- They survive moments but never build systems.

- They think deliverance is the end — but it's only the beginning.

- They need to call for reinforcement sometimes. Especially when weary. The enemy has a whole network and system, do not try to go it alone, every time.

The Secret: Fight Battles, but *Manage* War

- Wisdom is a war weapon
- Sabbaths are a war weapon
- Boundaries are a war weapon
- Silence is a war weapon
- Reinforcements and Godly human connections are weapons.

If you think it's a battle, you pray for victory.

If you know it's a war, you pray for strategy.

Battle versus War — Seeing the Bigger Conflict

You are not tired because you're weak. You are tired because you thought it was a fight — but hell declared a campaign.

Discernment would have told you that, or spiritual mapping—when you see that you are still fighting the same war that your father and his ancestors didn't fight, finish, or win. I'm speaking of ancestral curses such as poverty, sickness, lack, rage, anti-marriage, and other things that the family has endured generation after generation.

The enemy uses both battles and war in bringing conflict to the saints of God. Battles require courage, but wars require **systems, rest, boundaries and rotation. Even** Moses needed Aaron & Hur to hold up his arms.

Declarations:

- I will not survive moments and fail in seasons.
- I will not be strong in crisis but broken in consistency.
- I will not be a warrior with no strategy.
- I win the war, not just the fight.

Battle versus War

You're Not Losing. Don't Misread the Fight.

Are you exhausted? You are not exhausted because you are weak. You are exhausted because you thought it was a *battle*, but hell launched a *war*. You rebuked a moment, but the enemy scheduled a cycle. You shouted victory; but the enemy shifted to strategy. You thought you were done fighting but the enemy never left the field.

Most Christians know how to fight a battle, but we must learn how to win a war. Else even Christians could be celebrating breakthroughs and deliverances that they do not keep. Even Christians may survive attacks, but never recover from them. We must defeat enemies and outlast them, in the Name of Jesus.

- A battle tests your strength.
- A war tests your stamina, Wisdom, discipline, identity, and consistency.

First: Stop Fighting Battles God Never Called You To.

Discerning the conflict is critical first step. We must learn to see the big picture, the bigger conflict. The sooner, the better.

Some are losing not for being weak, or unconnected, or because you can't get a certain person to pray for you. A person could be losing if they are not supposed to be in a battle in the first place. Some are fighting battles God never assigned. Sadly, while doing this, they may be ignoring the war that God actually called you to win. Swinging swords in the wrong direction won't win anything.

Some are praying in the wrong dimension--, exhausted because of spending strength on current events while the enemy is playing for eras and generations ahead.

Too many think they are under attack, but they are actually under strategy. You thought you fought a demon, but you only fought a moment.

You shouted "VICTORY!" in a battle that was never the real war. It was a decoy.

Then the enemy smiled, because you celebrated too early.

Here are some key differences to be aware of. A clash in battle is a campaign in a war. A moment in a battle is a season in war. What is visible in a battle may be invisible in war. That which is temporary in a battle may be ongoing strategy in war. A battle may require courage, while a war requires endurance and Wisdom. Running a sprint requires something different than running a marathon.

A person could win a battle and still lose the war. That's why some people defeat the enemy once, but still end up defeated over time. Celebrate the Lord, not yourself when you win. Don't get too assured.

Here are some biblical examples of the battle being won but the war was still active.

David & Goliath — *Battle won,* But with Saul? That was a **war**. David fought Goliath with a stone. He survived Saul with strategy, discernment, restraint, and endurance.

Elijah & the Prophets of Baal — *Battle won.* But Jezebel? That was a **war of exhaustion**. Fire fell from heaven. Four hundred and fifty of Jezebel's prophets were defeated. The nation repented. But Jezebel whispered one threat… and the prophet of fire ran into depression, ran away into hiding in a cave. Because Jezebel didn't fight with swords. She fought with *wearing down*.

Jesus versus Satan in the Wilderness — *Battle won.* But Scripture says: *"And the devil left Him until an opportune time."* (Luke 4:13). That means the war wasn't over. Jesus knew that. The Cross was not a new attack; it was the next phase of the same war.

The enemy rarely wants a battle — he wants a pattern. The best two out of three—the rematch—that is the devil's idea, surely.

Battles drain fast. Wars drain slowly.

The enemy is not just trying to hurt you, he is trying to wear you down until you surrender willingly. The devil is spirit, he doesn't get tired. He recruits evil human agents who may tire, but then he will just get another one. Haven't you noticed that the thing, the situation, the battle you ran away from, another person will arise in your life to bring the same battle?

That's why the Enemy uses:

- Delays
- Cycles
- Attrition and draining people
- Emotional fatigue
- Repeated false accusations
- Subtle erosion of faith, focus, identity & passion--

Not to kill you, but to empty you. If the devil can't stop you in a clash, he will try to wear you out in a campaign.

The real reason many believers are tired is because they keep praying for battle strength when they really need war strategy. They want a miracle, while God is trying to give them management. They want *deliverance*, when they actually need d*iscipline*. They keep asking the same questions. "Are we there yet?" Or, "Why isn't this OVER yet?" Even if it is over, we have to **change** to keep the deliverance, to keep the victory. We can't go back to what we were doing before or a worse problem will come up against us. That's because of not being in a battle, but instead, being in a war. You're in a war.

Wars are not won by emotional surges. They are won by capacity, continuity, clarity, and consecrated rest.

YOU FIGHT BATTLES.
BUT YOU MUST *MANAGE* WAR.

You don't rebuke your way through war. You **build your way** through war.

- Rest is a war weapon.
- Rotation is a war weapon.
- Boundaries are a war weapon.
- Silence is a war weapon.
- Strategy is a war weapon.
- Knowing what to walk away from is a war weapon.

Some may be losing not because the devil is strong, but because they need **to stop swinging long enough to heal, plan, reset, get reinforcements, or hear God clearly.**

War requires wisdom, delegation, timing, systems, and endurance. Even Moses had to sit down and let Aaron and Hur hold up his arms. That wasn't weakness. That was warfare intelligence.

Reflection Questions

1. **Where have I been celebrating "victory" even though the war is still active?**
2. **Where am I exhausted because I'm fighting what God never assigned me to fight?**
3. **Where do I need strategy instead of strength?**
4. **What long-term cycles have I mistaken for isolated attacks?**
5. **Am I asking God for miracles in places where He's requiring structure?**

PROPHETIC DECLARATION

- I will win moments and seasons, in the Name of Jesus.

- I will not fight everything that calls me.
- I will not fight where there is no prize.
- I will not confuse noise with assignment.
- I will not give energy to battles that do not advance destiny.
- I am not just a warrior — I am a strategist.
- I win wars, not just fights. In Jesus' Name."

War Strategy Activation Prayer

Lord, open my eyes. Show me where I am battling out of emotion when I should be governing with Wisdom.

Lord, teach me to see the campaign, not just the clash. Give me insight, timing, strategy, and rest.

Break the illusion of urgency. Break the addiction to constant fighting. Train me to win long-term, not just loud.

Make me a commander, not just a soldier. Make me victorious not just in battle — but in destiny.

In the Name of Jesus. Amen.

Scriptural Warfare Against Enemies

1. Thy right hand, O LORD, is become glorious in power: thy right hand, O LORD, hath dashed in pieces the enemy. (Exodus 15:6)

2. The enemy said, I will pursue, I will overtake, I will divide the spoil; my lust shall be satisfied upon them; I will draw my sword, my hand shall destroy them. (Exodus 15:9)

3. Lord, be an enemy to all my enemies and an adversary to all my adversaries. (see Exodus 23:22)

4. Lord, I blow an alarm with the trumpets as I go to war in my land against the enemy that oppresses me, and Lord, let me be

remembered before You and let me be saved from my enemies, in the Name of Jesus. (Numbers 10:9)

5. Lord, make Your arrows drunk with the blood of my enemies, let Your sword devour flesh, and as You exact revenge upon the enemy (see Deuteronomy 32:42)

6. The eternal God *is* *thy* refuge, and underneath *are* the everlasting arms: and he shall thrust out the enemy from before thee; and shall say, Destroy *them*. (Deuteronomy 33:27)

7. We praise You, Lord God for, Our God hath delivered into our hands our enemy and the destroyer of our country, which slew man of us. (see Judges 16:24)

8. Lord, deal with all my continual, unrelenting, perpetual, unrepentant enemies, in the Name of Jesus. (see 1 Samuel 18:29)

9. Lord, do not depart from me; continually be an enemy to my enemy, in the Name of Jesus. (1 Samuel 28:16)

10. Lord, deliver me from my strong enemy, and from them that hated me; for they were too strong for me. (2 Samuel 22:18)

11. Lord, let me be strong for the battle, Lord, You have power to help and power to cast down my enemy. Help me, Lord, in the Name of Jesus. (see 2 Chronicles 25:8)

12. Lord, send help to me against the enemy, in the Name of Jesus.

13. Lord, we seek You; let Your hand be upon us for good. Send forth help from the sanctuary against the enemy, in the Name of Jesus. (see Ezra 8:22)

14. Lord, deliver me from the hand of the enemy, that is hidden and lays in wait, in the Name of Jesus. (Ezra 8:31)

15. Lord deliver me from the adversary and the enemy and his wickedness, in the Name of Jesus. (see Esther 7:6)

16. Lord, you know my enemies; destroy the power that animates them, that empowers them, that influences them against me, in the Name of Jesus.

17. Father, by Your finger, deliver me from the wrath of the enemy that hates me, that desires to tear me, gnash me with his teeth and that sharpens his eye upon me, in the Name of Jesus. (see Job 16:19)

18. Out of the mouth of babes and sucklings hast thou ordained strength because of thing enemies, that though mightiest still the enemy and the avenger. (Psalm 8:2)

19. Lord, do not let my enemies be exalted over me, in the Name of Jesus. (Psalm 13:2)

20. He delivered me from my strong enemy, and from them which hated

me: for they were too strong for me. (Psalm 18:17)

21. Lord, free me from the hand and the land of the enemy in the Name of Jesus.

22. By this I know that You favor me, Lord because you did not let my enemy triumph over me. (Psalm 41:11)

23. For thou *art* the God of my strength. Deliver me from the hand of the enemy, in the Name of Jesus. (see Psalm 43:2)

24. For thou hast been a shelter for me, *and* a strong tower from the enemy. (Psalm 61:3)

25. Hear my voice, O God, in my prayer: preserve my life from fear of the enemy. (Psalm 64:1)

26. Lord, let the enemy not exact upon me, nor the son of wickedness afflict me, in the Name of Jesus. (see Psalm 89:22)

27. And he saved them from the hand of him that hated *them*, and redeemed them from the hand of the enemy. (Psalm 106:10)

28. Let the redeemed of the Lord say so, whom he hath redeemed from the hand of the enemy; (Psalm 107:2)

29. So shall they fear the name of the LORD from the west, and his glory from the rising of the sun. When the enemy shall come in like a flood, the Spirit of the LORD shall lift up a standard against him. (Isaiah 59:19)

30. Lord, scatter my enemies as with an east wind; show them your back and not Your face, in the Name of Jesus. (see Jeremiah 18:17)

31. Lord, do not let my enemies rejoice over me, guard and protect Your investment in me, in the Name of Jesus.

32. Rejoice not against me, O mine enemy: when I fall, I shall arise; when I sit in

darkness, the LORD *shall be* a light unto me. (Micah 7:8)

33. Lord, let my enemy be covered in shame and trodden down as the mire in the streets, in the Name of Jesus. (see Micah 7:10)

34. Lord, cast out my enemy, so I do not see evil anymore, in the Name of Jesus. (Zephaniah 3:15)

35. Lord, I receive power to tread on serpents, and scorpions, and over all the power of the enemy: and nothing shall by any means hurt me. (Luke 10:19)

36. The last enemy that was destroyed is death; Lord let the enemies who seek after my life, instead of me, let them be destroyed, in the Name of Jesus. (1 Corinthians 15:26)

37. I seal these words decrees, declarations and prayers across every dimension and timeline, past, present, and future, to infinity, in the Name of Jesus.

38. I seal them with the Blood of Jesus and the Holy Spirit of Promise.

39. Any retaliation against this speaker, listener, or anyone who prays these prayers, makes these decrees and declarations at any time, let that retaliation backfire on the head of the perpetrator to infinity and without Mercy, in the Name of Jesus.

AMEN.

Dear Reader

Thank you for reading this book. I pray it enlightened you to the end of successful warfare battles and campaigns, in the Name of Jesus.

Shalom, Dr. Marlene Miles

There is a workbook with Leader's Guide to accompany the book you have just read. It is

entitled, **KNOW YOUR BATTLE: The Workbook:
Stop Swinging Blindly — and Win Against
Opponents, Adversaries & Enemies**

Prayerbooks by this author

While most books by this author have prayer points either throughout the book or at the end, there are some books that are only prayers. You just open up the book and pray.

Prayers Against Barrenness: *For Success in Business and Life*

Fruit of the Womb: *Prayers Against Barrenness*

Beauty Curses, *Warfare Prayers Against*
https://a.co/d/5Xlc20M

Courts of Marriage: Prayers for Marriage in the Courts of Heaven *(prayerbook)*
https://a.co/d/cNAdgAq

Courtroom Warfare @ Midnight *(prayerbook)*
https://a.co/d/5fc7Qdp

Demonic Cobwebs *(prayerbook)* https://a.co/d/fp9Oa2H

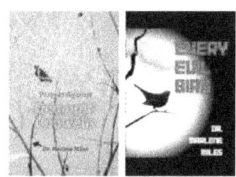

Every Evil Bird https://a.co/d/hF1kh1O

Gates of Thanksgiving

Spirits of Death, Hell & the Grave, Pass Over Me and My House

Throne of Grace: Courtroom Prayer

Warfare Prayer Against Poverty
https://a.co/d/bZ61lYu

Other books by this author

200 RED FLAGS: THE TRACK IS NOT SAFE

AK: The Adventures of the Agape Kid

Already Married in the Spirit: *Why You May Not Be Married in the Natural*

AMONG SOME THIEVES https://a.co/d/dkYT4ZV

Ancestral Powers

Anti-Marriage, *The Spirit of* https://a.co/d/fEKrHFu

Backstabbers https://a.co/d/gi8iBxf

Barrenness, *Prayers Against* https://a.co/d/feUltIs

Battlefield of Marriage, *The*

Beware of the Dog: Prayers Against Dogs in the Dream.

Bless Your Food: *Let the Dining Table be Undefiled*

Blindsided: *Has the Old Man Bewitched You?* https://a.co/d/5O2fLLR

Break Free from Collective Captivity
Broken Spirits & Dry Bones
By Means of a Whorish Father
Caged Life: Get Out Alive!
https://a.co/d/bwPbksX

Casting Down Imaginations
Churchzilla, The Wanna-Be, Supposed-to-be Bride of Christ
Demonic Cobwebs (prayerbook)
Demonic Time Bombs
Demons Hate Questions
Devil Loves Trauma, *The*
Devil Weapons: Unforgiveness, Bitterness,…
The Devourers: Thieves of Darkness 2
Do Not Swear by the Moon
Don't Refuse Me, Lord (4 book series)
https://a.co/d/idP34LG
Dream Defilement

The Emptiers: *Thieves of Darkness,* 1
https://a.co/d/5I4n5mc

Evil Touch

Failed Assignment

Fantasy Spirit Spouse https://a.co/d/hW7oYbX

FAT Demons (The): *Breaking Demonic Curses*
https://a.co/d/4kP8wV1

The Fold (5-book series)

1. The Fold (Book 1)
2. Name Your Seed (Book 2)
3. The Poor Attitudes of Money (3)
4. Do Not Orphan Your Seed (4)
5. For the Sake of the Gospel (5)
6. My Sowing Journal

Gang Ups: Touch Not God's Anointed

Getting Rid of Evil Spiritual Food

https://a.co/d/i2L3WYQ

got HEALING? Verses for Life

got LOVE? Verses for Life

got HOPE? Verses for Life

got money? https://a.co/d/g2av41N

Has My Soul Been Sold?
https://a.co/d/dyB8hhA

Here Come the Horns: *Skilled to Destroy*
https://a.co/d/cZiNnkP

Hidden Sins: Hidden Iniquity
https://a.co/d/4Mth0wa

How to Dental Assist

How to Dental Assist2: Be Productive, Not Wasteful

How to STOP Being a Blind Witch or Warlock

I Take It Back

Legacy

Let Me Have A Dollar's Worth
https://a.co/d/h8F8XgE

Level the Playing Field

Living for the NOW of God

Lose My Location https://a.co/d/crD6mV9

Love Breaks Your Heart

Made Perfect In Love

Mammon https://a.co/d/29yhMG7

Man Safari, *The*

Marriage Ed. Rules of Engagement & Marriage

Made Perfect in Love

Money Hunters: Beware of Those

Money on the Altar https://a.co/d/4EqJ2Nr

Mulberry Tree, *The* https://a.co/d/9nR9rRb

Motherboard (The) - *Soul Prosperity Series*

Name Your Seed

Occupy: *Until I Return* https://a.co/d/bZ7ztUy

Opponent, Adversary, or Enemy?: Fight The Right Battle with the Right Weapons

Plantation Souls

Players Gonna Play

Portals: Shut the Front Door: Prayers to Close Evil Portals.

Power Money: Nine Times the Tithe

https://a.co/d/gRt41gy

The Power to Get Wealth

https://a.co/d/e4ub4Ov

Powers Above

The Robe, Part 1, The Lessons of Joseph

The Robe, Part II, The Lessons of Joseph

Seasons of Grief

Seasons of Waiting

Seasons of War

Second Marriage, Third--, *Any Marriage*

https://a.co/d/6m6GN4N

Seducing Spirits: Idolatry & Whoredoms

https://a.co/d/4Jq4WEs

Shut the Front Door: *Prayers to Close Portals*

https://a.co/d/cH4TWJj

Sift You Like Wheat

Six Men Short: What Has Happened to all the Men?

SLAVE

Sleep Afflictions & Really Bad Dreams
https://a.co/d/f8sDmgv

Soul Prosperity soul prosperity series 3

https://a.co/d/5p8YvCN

Souls Captivity soul prosperity series 2

The Spirit of Anti-Marriage

The Spirit of Poverty https://a.co/d/abV2o2e

Spiritual Thieves https://a.co/d/eqPPz33

StarStruck~ Triangular Power series.

SUNBLOCK~ Triangular Power series.

The Swallowers: *Thieves of Darkness*, 3

Take It Back

This Is NOT That: How to Keep Demons from Coming at You

Time Is of the Essence

Too Many Wives: *Why You Have Lady Problems*

Tormenting Spirits   https://a.co/d/dAogEJf

Toxic Souls

Triangular Power *(series)*, Powers Above, SUNBLOCK, Do Not Swear by the Moon, STARSTRUCK

Unbreak My Heart: *Don't Let Me Die*

Uncontested Doom

Unguarded Hours, *The*

Unseen Life, *The* (forthcoming)

Upgrade: How to Get Out of Survival Mode Toxic Souls (Book 2 of series) , Legacy (Book 3 of series)

The Wasters: *Thieves of Darkness*, Bk 2
https://a.co/d/bUvI9Jo

What Have You to Declare? What Do You Have With You from Where You've Been?

When I Was A Child, *I Prayed As a Child*

When the Devourer is Rebuked

https://a.co/d/1HVv8oq

Why Do I Keep Meeting the Same Guy?

https://a.co/d/0BcAWmW

WTH? Get Me Out of This Hell
https://a.co/d/a7WBGJh

The Wilderness Romance *(series)* This series is about conducting a Godly relationship and marriage with someone who is a Wilderness person. It is about how to recognize it and navigate through it.

These books are about how not to get caught up in such.

- *The Social Wilderness*
- *The Sexual Wilderness*
- *The Spiritual Wilderness*

Other Series

The Fold (a series on Godly finances)
https://a.co/d/4hz3unj

Soul Prosperity Series https://a.co/d/bz2M42q

Spirit Spouse books

https://a.co/d/9VehDSo

https://a.co/d/97sKOwm

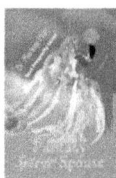

Battlefield of Marriage, The

https://a.co/d/eUDzizO

Players Gonna Play

https://a.co/d/2hzGw3N

Sent Spirit Spouse (can someone send you a spirit spouse? This book is not yet released.)

Matters of the Heart, Made Perfect in Love

https://a.co/d/7OMQW3O , Love Breaks Your Heart https://a.co/d/4KvuQLZ, Unbreak My Heart https://a.co/d/84ceZ6M Broken Spirits & Dry Bones https://a.co/d/e6iedNP

Thieves of Darkness series

The Emptiers https://a.co/d/heio0dO

The Wasters https://a.co/d/5TG1iNQ

The Swallowers https://a.co/d/1jWhM6G

The Devourers: Why We Can't Have Nice Things https://a.co/d/87Tejbf

Spiritual Thieves

Triangular Powers https://a.co/d/aUCjAWC 4-book series.

Upgrade (series) *How to Get Out of Survival Mode*
https://a.co/d/aTERhXO

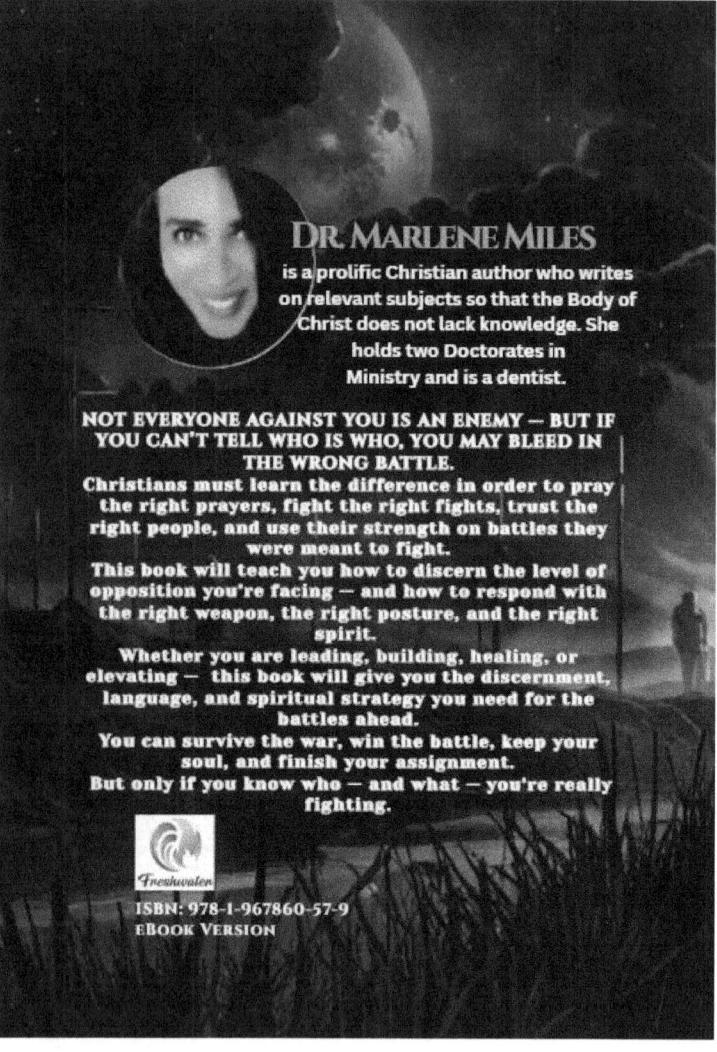

www.ingramcontent.com/pod-product-compliance
Lightning Source LLC
LaVergne TN
LVHW051245080426
835513LV00016B/1744